Grade 4   Level 4 Early inter

Improve your sight-reading!

Paul Harris

Stage 1   **Playing musically**

Stage 2   **Simple syncopations**

Stage 3   ♫♫

Stage 4   6/8   ♩. ♩ ♪   ♫♫

Stage 5   **More chords**

Stage 6   **More rhythms in** 6/8

Stage 7   ♫♫ and ♫♫

Stage 8   **More rhythms in** 3/8

Stage 9   **Revision of keys and rhythms**

FABER ff MUSIC

Practice chart

	Comments (from you, your teacher or parent)	Done!
Stage 1		
Stage 2		
Stage 3		
Stage 4		
Stage 5		
Stage 6		
Stage 7		
Stage 8		
Stage 9		

Teacher's name _____

Telephone _____

Many thanks to Jean Cockburn, Claire Dunham, Graeme Humphrey and Diana Jackson for their invaluable help, and particular thanks to Lesley Rutherford whose editorial skills and perpetual encouragement went far beyond the call of duty.

© 2008 by Faber Music Ltd.
This edition first published in 2008 by Faber Music Ltd.
Bloomsbury House, 74–77 Great Russell Street, London WC1B 3DA
Music setting by Graham Pike
Cover and page design by Susan Clarke
Cover illustration by Drew Hillier
Printed in England by Caligraving Ltd
All rights reserved

ISBN10: 0-571-53304-3 (US edition 0-571-53314-0)
EAN13: 978-0-571-53304-6 (US edition 978-0-571-53314-5)

To buy Faber Music publications or to find out about the full range of titles available please contact your local music retailer or Faber Music sales enquiries:
Faber Music Ltd, Burnt Mill, Elizabeth Way, Harlow CM20 2HX
Tel: +44 (0) 1279 82 89 82   Fax: +44 (0) 1279 82 89 83
sales@fabermusic.com   fabermusic.com

Introduction

Being a good sight-reader is so important and it needn't be difficult! If you work through this book carefully – always making sure that you really understand each exercise before you play it, you'll never have problems learning new pieces or doing well at sight-reading in exams!

Using the workbook

1 Rhythmic exercises
Make sure you have grasped these fully before you go on to the melodic exercises: it is vital that you really know how the rhythms work. There are a number of ways to do these examples – see *Improve your sight-reading* Grade 1 for more details.

2 Melodic exercises
These exercises use just the notes and rhythms for the Stage, and also give some help with fingering. If you want to sight-read fluently and accurately, get into the habit of working through each exercise in the following ways before you begin to play it:
- Make sure you understand the rhythm and counting. Clap the exercise through.
- Look at the shape of the tune, particularly the highest and lowest notes and think about the best way to finger it.
- Try to hear the piece through in your head. Always play the first note to help.

3 Prepared pieces
Work your way through the questions first, as these will help you to think about or 'prepare' the piece. Don't begin playing until you are pretty sure you know exactly how the piece goes.

4 Going solo!
It is now up to you to discover the clues in this series of practice pieces. Give yourself about a minute and do your best to understand the piece before you play. Check the rhythms and hand position, and try to hear the piece in your head.

Always remember to feel the pulse and to keep going steadily once you've begun.

Good luck and happy sight-reading!

Terminology:
Bar = measure

Stage 1

Playing musically

Whenever you speak you put expression into what you say. Do the same with your sight-reading performances! As you're preparing the piece, as well as thinking about the notes, shape and rhythm, think about how you'll interpret the piece – or play it musically. You will need to think about:

- Does it require crisp or more gentle and sustained playing?
- Do you need to use accents in addition to those that are marked?
- Is it a tune with accompaniment? (Balance of hands will be important if so.)
- Are both hands equally important?
- What would be an effective speed?

Rhythmic exercises

Always count two bars before you begin each exercise – one out loud and one silently.

Melodic exercises

Prepared pieces

1 What are the clues to the character of this piece?
2 Should the notes be played *legato* or detached?
3 Think about your fingering and changing hand position.
4 Tap the rhythm of the piece, hands together.
5 Play the first note of each hand and then hear the piece in your head as best you can.
6 Do you feel confident that you'll give an accurate performance?

1 What are the main clues to the character of this piece?
2 What interval is formed by the first two notes of the left hand?
3 How many bars are based on scale and arpeggio patterns? (Play the scale and arpeggio.)
4 Look through the piece for changes of hand position.
5 Tap the rhythm of the piece, hands together.
6 Play the first note of each hand and then hear the piece in your head as best you can.

Stage 1

Going solo!

Don't forget to prepare each piece carefully before you play it.

Stage 2

Simple syncopations

Rhythmic exercises

Always count two bars before you begin each exercise – one out loud and one silently, then continue to feel the pulse strongly.

Melodic exercises

Don't forget to count two bars before you begin each melodic exercise as well.

Prepared pieces

> 1 What is the key of this piece? Play the scale and arpeggio.
>
> 2 Are there any repeated patterns?
>
> 3 What does 'swing the quavers' mean? Tap the rhythm of each hand separately. Now tap the rhythms of both hands together.
>
> 4 Look carefully for changes of hand position in the right hand. How many are there?
>
> 5 Look at the final chord in the right hand. Now play it.
>
> 6 Play the first note in each hand and hear the piece in your head as best you can.

> 1 What is the key of this piece? Play the scale and arpeggio.
>
> 2 Where does the right hand change position?
>
> 3 Are there any repeated patterns?
>
> 4 Clap the left hand and think the right hand silently.
>
> 5 Can you spot any patterns based on scales?
>
> 6 Play the first note in each hand and hear the piece in your head as best you can.

Stage 2

Going solo!

Stage 3

Rhythmic exercises

Always count two bars before you begin each exercise – one out loud and one silently.

Melodic exercises

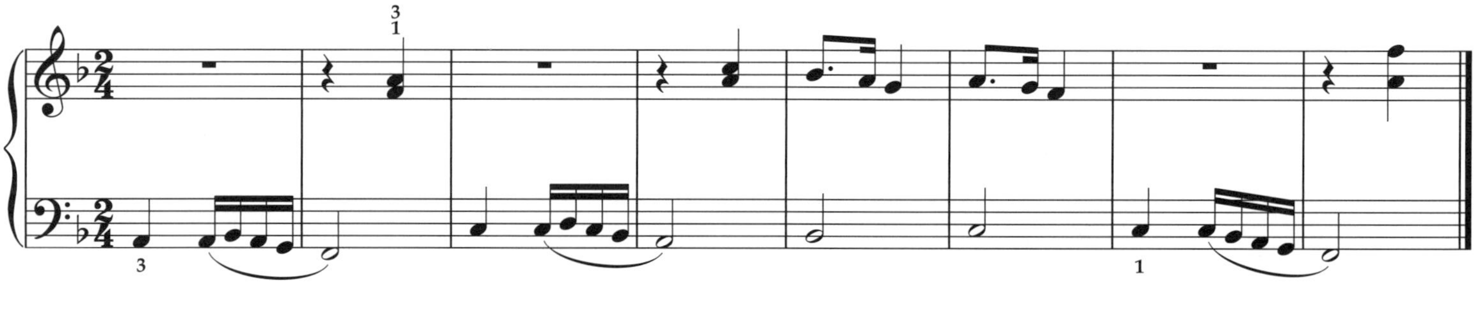

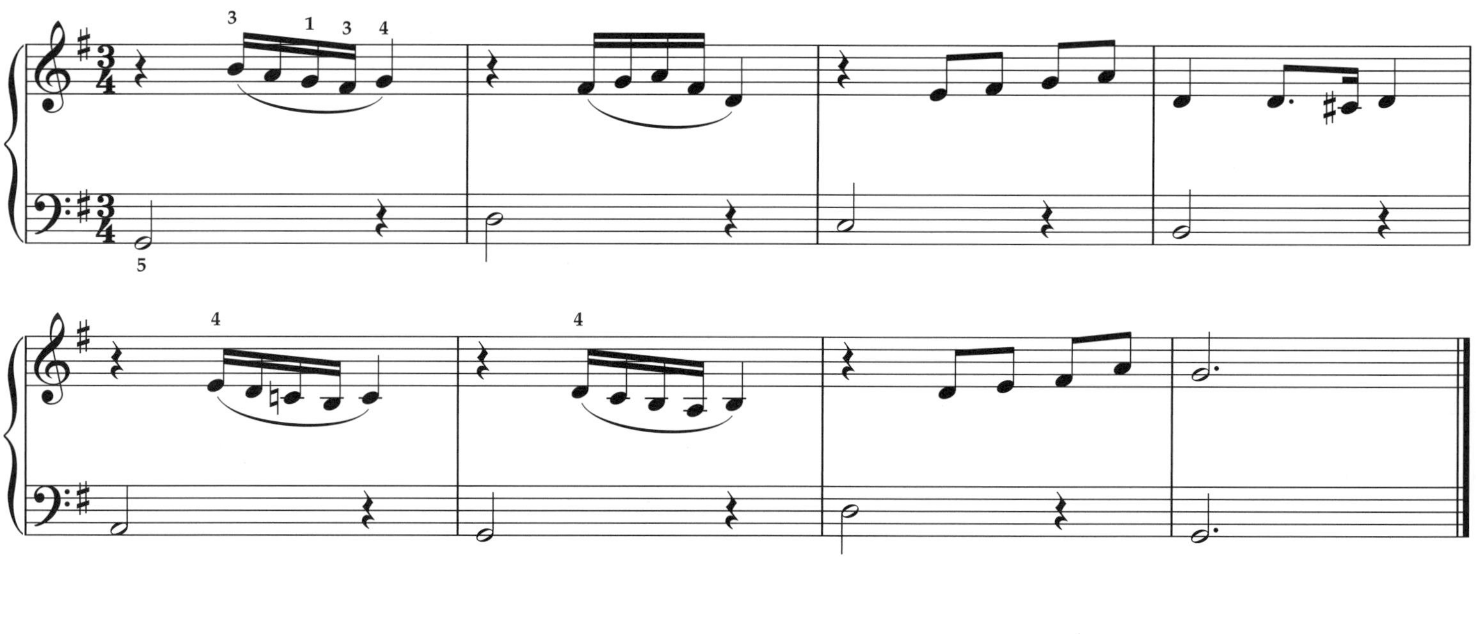

Stage 3

Prepared pieces

> 1 What is the key of this piece? Play the scale and arpeggio.
> 2 Think how you will finger the chords in bars 1–4 and bars 7-8 (left hand).
> 3 Are there any repeated patterns?
> 4 What will you count? Tap the rhythm of each hand separately then both together.
> 5 Play the first note of each hand and then hear the piece through in your head.
> 6 How will you give a waltz-like performance?

> 1 What is the key of this piece? Play the scale and arpeggio.
> 2 Can you see any bars that are not based on scale or arpeggio patterns?
> 3 Search for the E flats and store them up in your mind.
> 4 How will the ♩♩♩♩ in the final bar affect your choice of tempo?
> 5 Tap the rhythm of each hand separately. Now tap the rhythms of both hands together.
> 6 How will you bring this piece to life?

Going solo!

Don't forget to prepare each piece carefully before you play it.

Stage 4

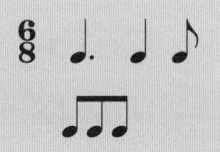

Rhythmic exercises

Always count two bars before you begin each exercise (one out loud and one silently), then continue to feel the pulse strongly.

1

2

3

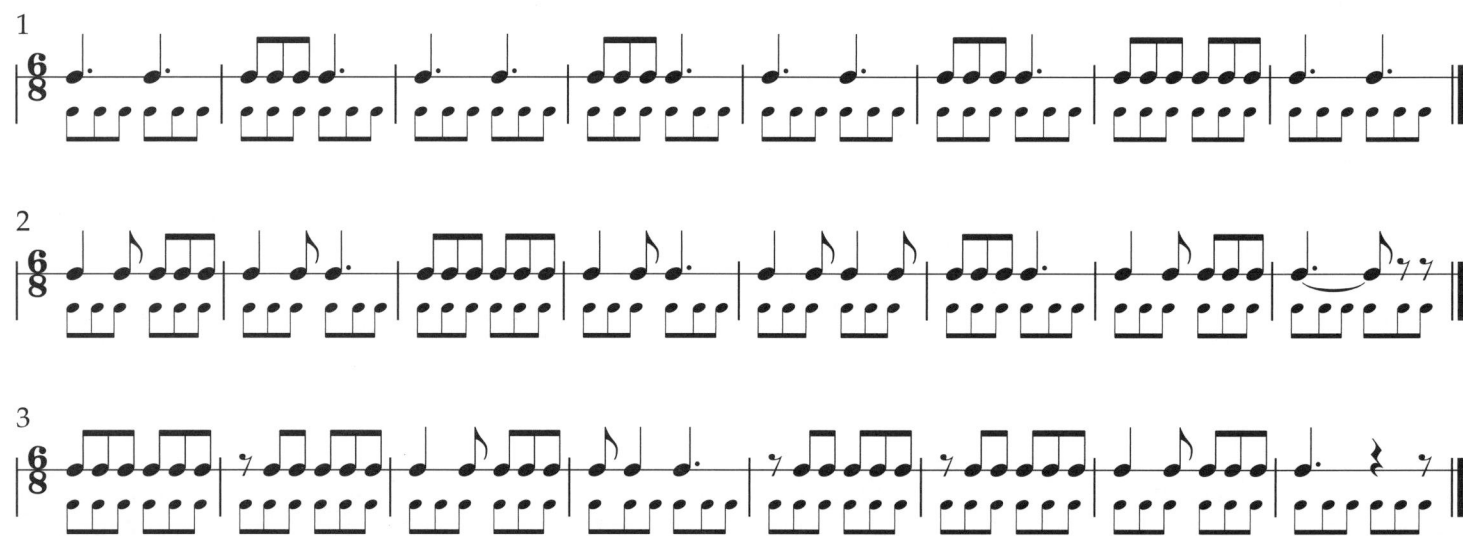

Melodic exercises

Don't forget to count two bars before you begin each melodic exercise as well.

1

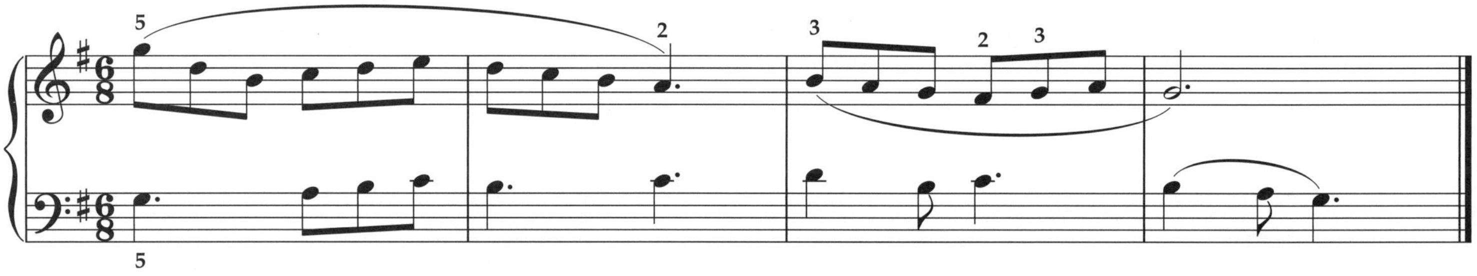

2

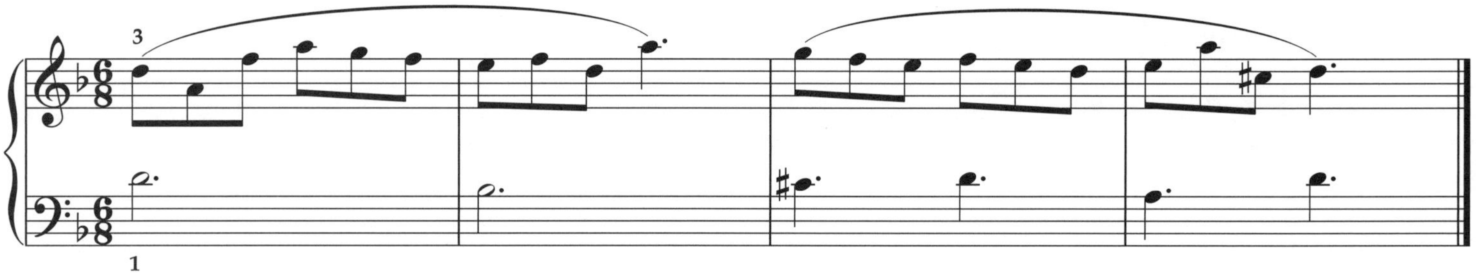

3

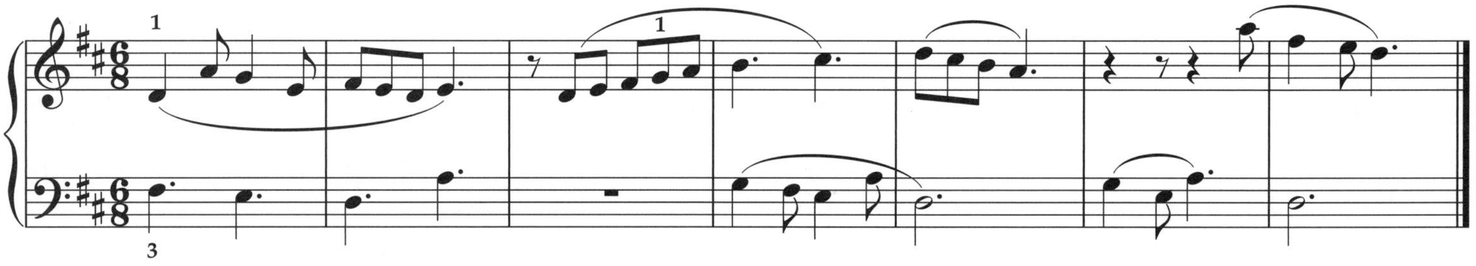

Stage 4

17

Prepared pieces

1. What is the key of this piece? Play the scale and arpeggio.
2. Are there any scale patterns?
3. What is a tarantella?
4. What will you count? Tap the rhythm of each hand separately then both hands together.
5. Play the first note of each hand and then hear the piece through in your head.
6. How will you give a characterful performance?

1. What is the key of this piece? Play the scale and arpeggio.
2. Which notes are affected by the key signature?
3. Is the melody mainly in the right or left hand?
4. What will you count? Tap the rhythms of each hand separately. Then tap the rhythm of both hands together.
5. Play the first note of each hand and then hear the piece through in your head.
6. How will you give your performance character?

Going solo!

Stage 5

More chords

Rhythmic exercises

Hear these rhythms in your head as well as clapping them.

1

2

3

Melodic exercises

Make sure you have a good idea of what each piece will sound like before you play it.

1

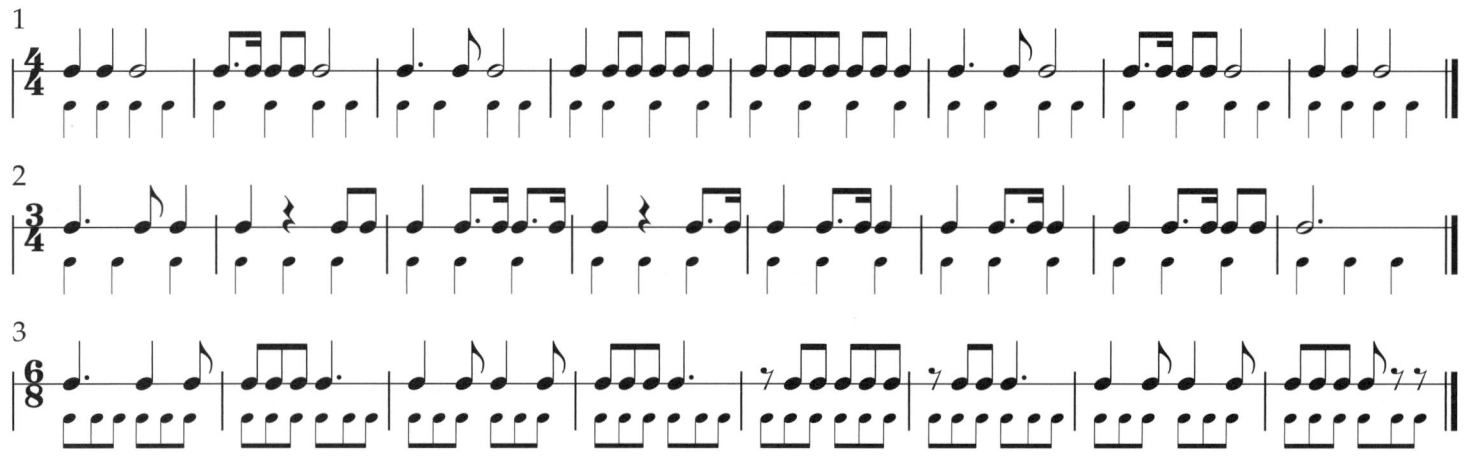

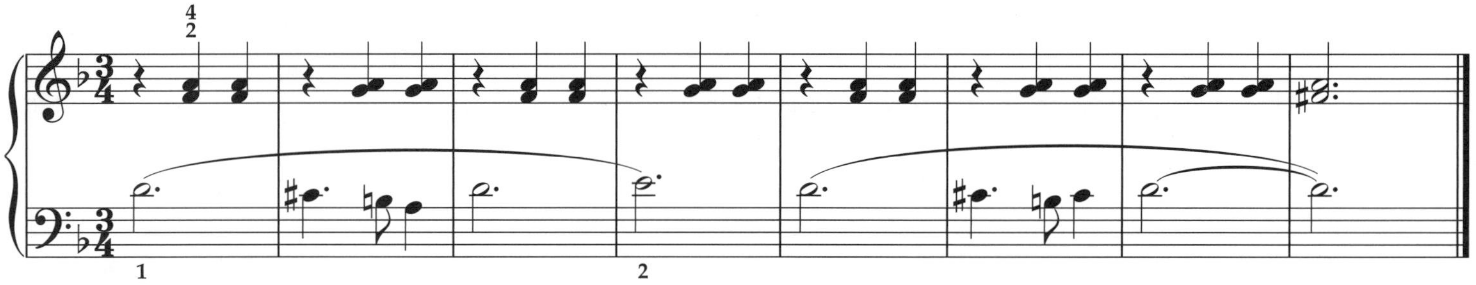

2

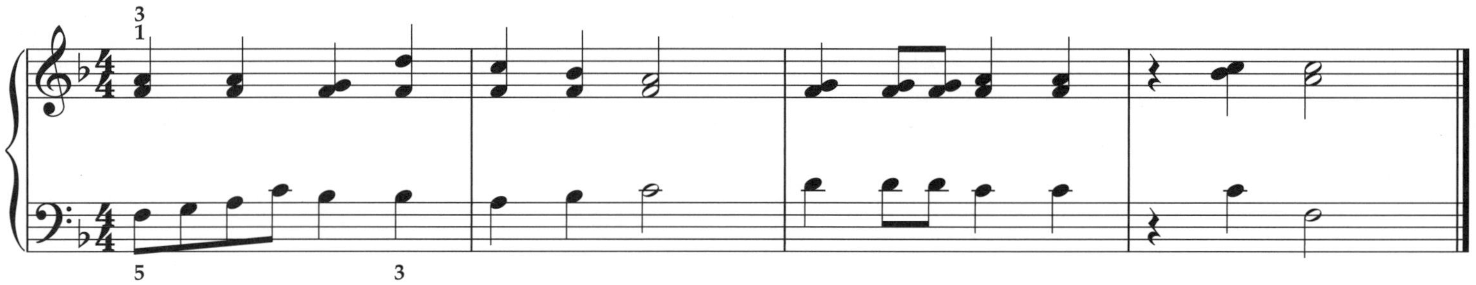

3

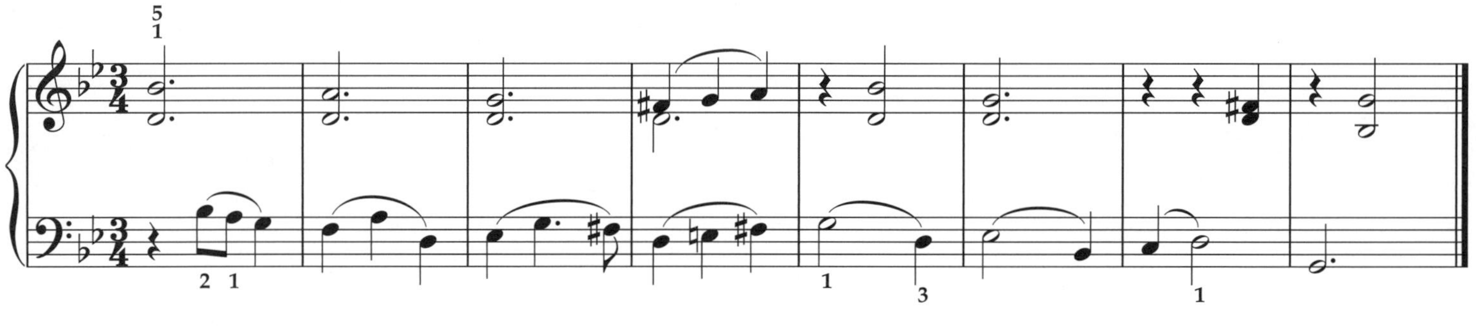

Stage 5

Prepared pieces

1. What is the key of this piece? Play the scale and arpeggio.
2. Play the tonic triad of the home key. Can you find that chord in the piece? (There are four appearances!)
3. Think about how you will finger the first four bars of the right hand.
4. Can you spot any repeated rhythmic patterns?
5. There is only one change of hand position necessary – where is it?
6. Play the first note in each hand and hear the piece in your head as best you can.

1. What is the key of this piece? Play the scale and arpeggio.
2. Where is the melody in this piece? Does it change hands?
3. Clap the left hand and think the right hand silently.
4. Can you spot any repeated patterns or patterns based on scales?
5. What does '*mesto*' mean? How will you give character to this piece?
6. Play the first note in each hand and hear the piece in your head as best you can.

Stage 5

Going solo!

Don't forget to prepare each piece carefully before you play it.

Stage 6

More rhythms in $\frac{6}{8}$

Rhythmic exercises

Always count two bars before you begin each exercise – one out loud and one silently.

1

2

3

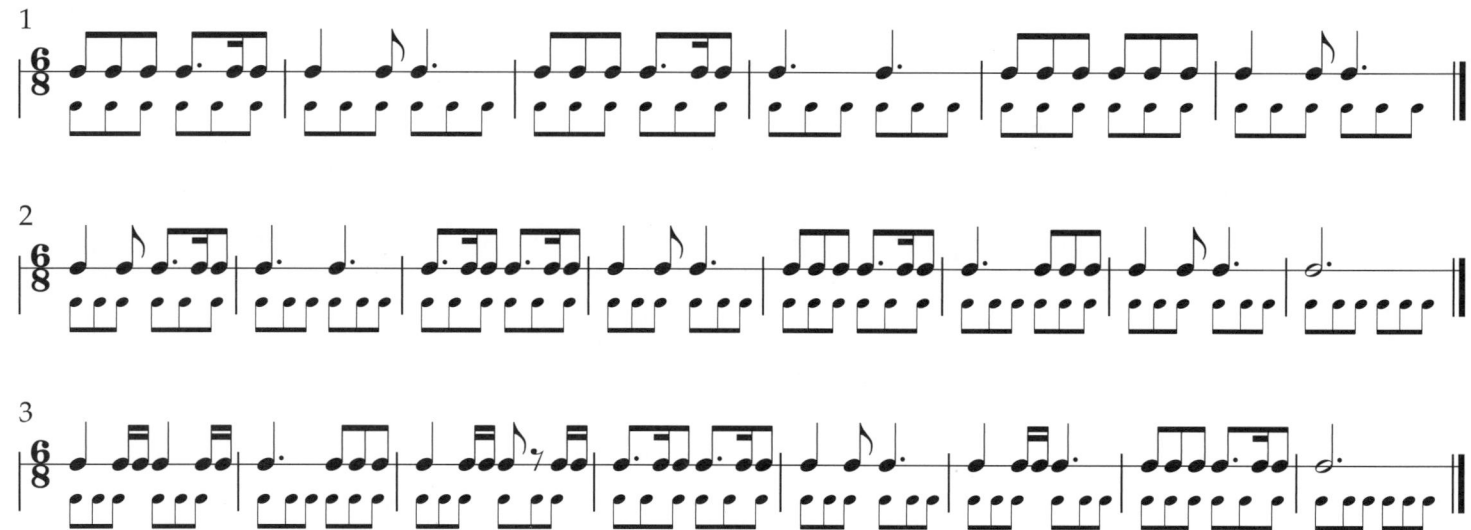

Melodic exercises

And don't forget to count two bars before you begin each melodic exercise as well.

1

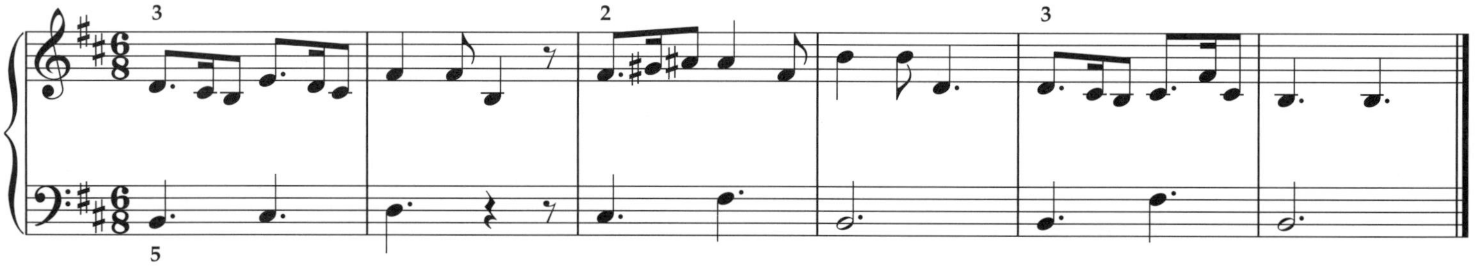

2

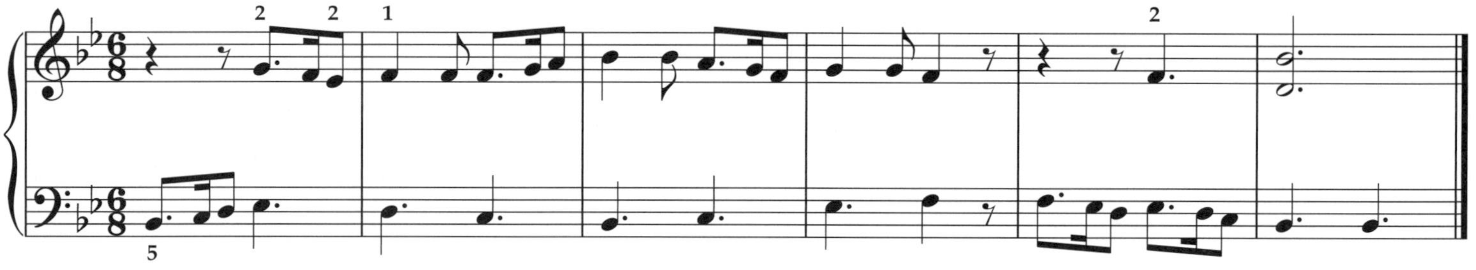

3

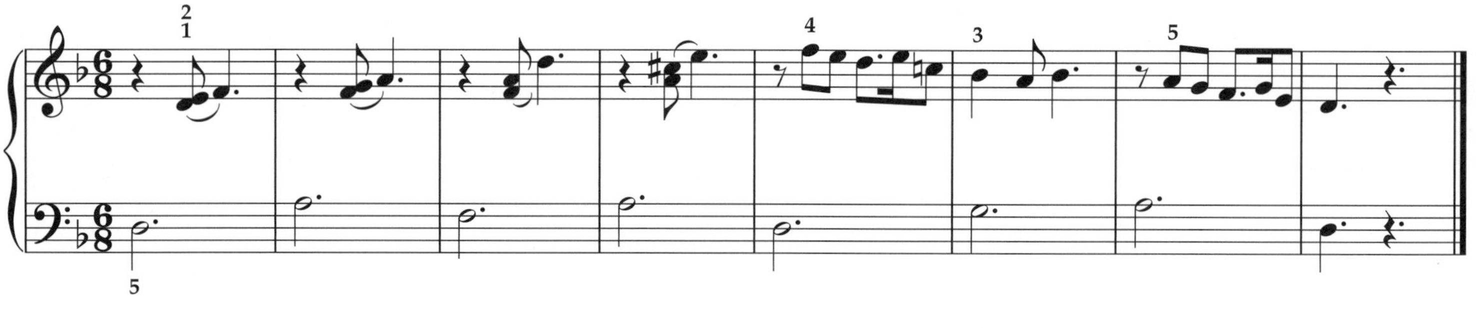

Prepared pieces

> 1 Which hand has the melody at the start of this piece?
> 2 What is the name of the second note in the left hand? What is another name for this note?
> 3 Can you spot any repeated patterns?
> 4 What will you count? Tap the rhythm of each hand separately then both together.
> 5 Which ingredients give you clues to the character of this piece?

> 1 Does the opening phrase return anywhere?
> 2 What does *Andante espressivo* suggest about the character?
> 3 Think about an appropriate speed and establish a strong pulse in your mind.
> 4 What will you count? Tap the rhythm of each hand separately then both together.
> 5 What key is the piece in? Play the scale and arpeggio.
> 6 Play the first note of each hand and then hear the piece in your head as best you can.

Stage 6

Going solo!

Stage 7

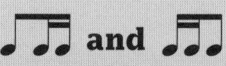

Rhythmic exercises

Clap the following two exercises many times over until you feel really confident you know how they go.

Melodic exercises

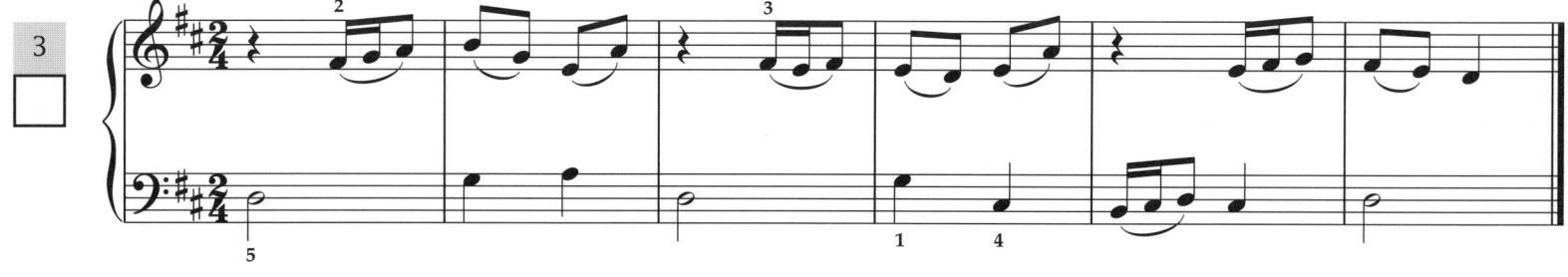

Stage 7

Prepared pieces

> 1. How many times does the opening rhythm (bar 1) return? Do you know exactly how it goes?
> 2. Which chord are bars 1 and 2 (right hand) based on?
> 3. What fingering will you use for the chords in the left hand, bars 1–3?
> 4. What key is this piece in? Play the scale and arpeggio.
> 5. What will you count? Tap the rhythms of each hand separately. Then tap the rhythm of both hands together.
> 6. What ingredients give you clues to the character of this piece?

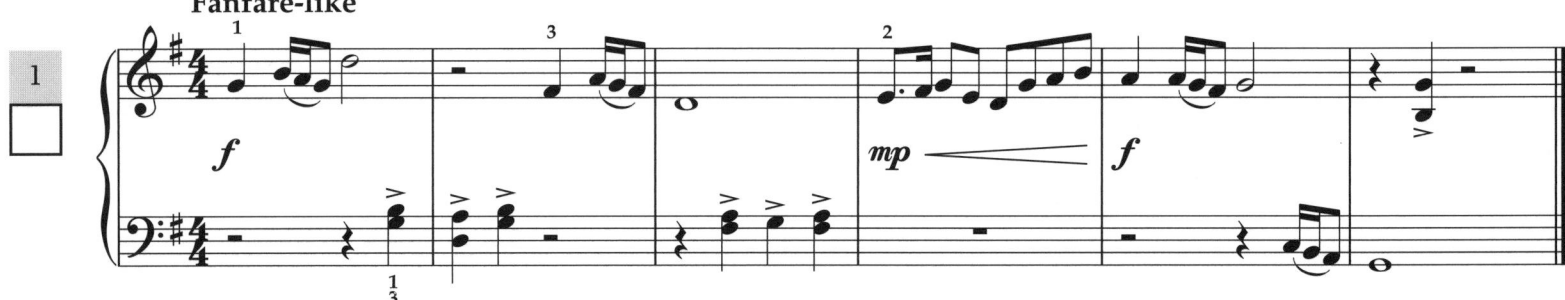

> 1. Tapping the pulse, hear the rhythm of both hands in your head.
> 2. Are there any changes of hand position?
> 3. How many times does the rhythm of bar 1 return?
> 4. What is the character of this piece?
> 5. What is the connection between the first left-hand chord and the first two right-hand notes?
> 6. Play the first note of each hand and then hear the piece in your head.

Going solo!

Don't forget to prepare each piece carefully before you play it.

Stage 8

More rhythms in 3/8

Rhythmic exercises

Always count two bars before you begin each exercise – one out loud and one silently then continue to feel the pulse strongly.

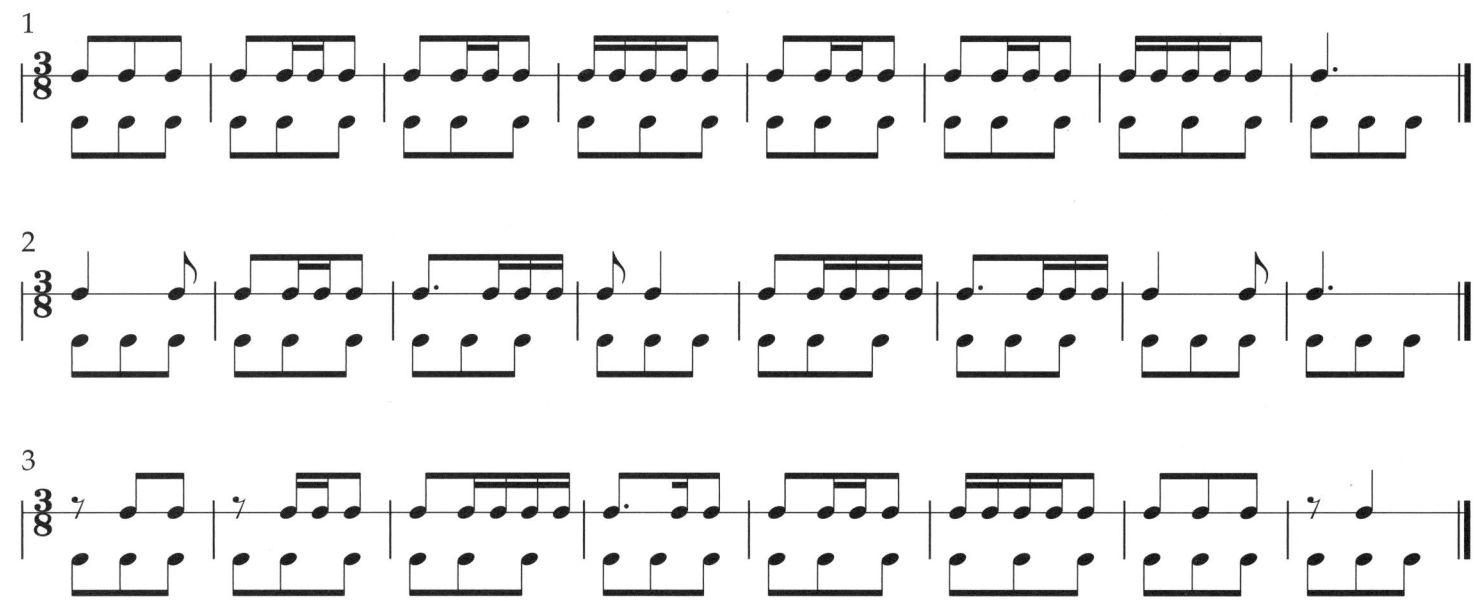

Melodic exercises

Don't forget to count two bars before you begin each melodic exercise as well.

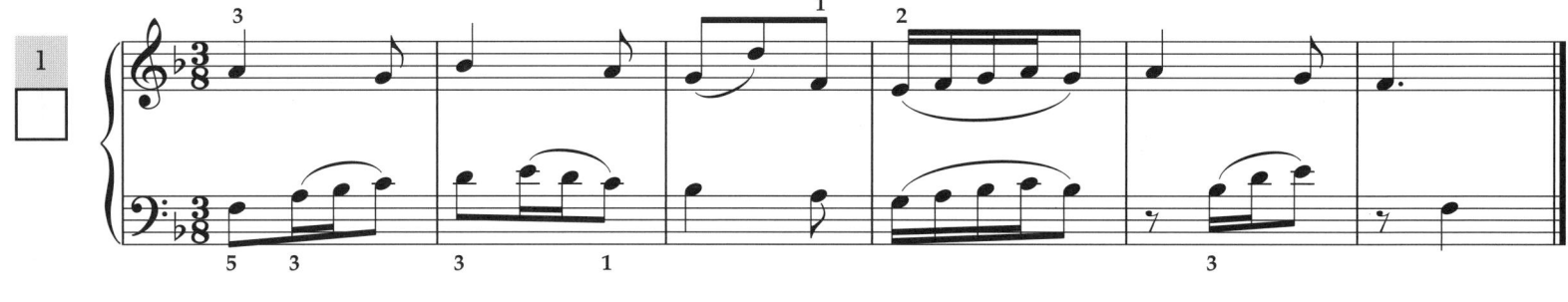

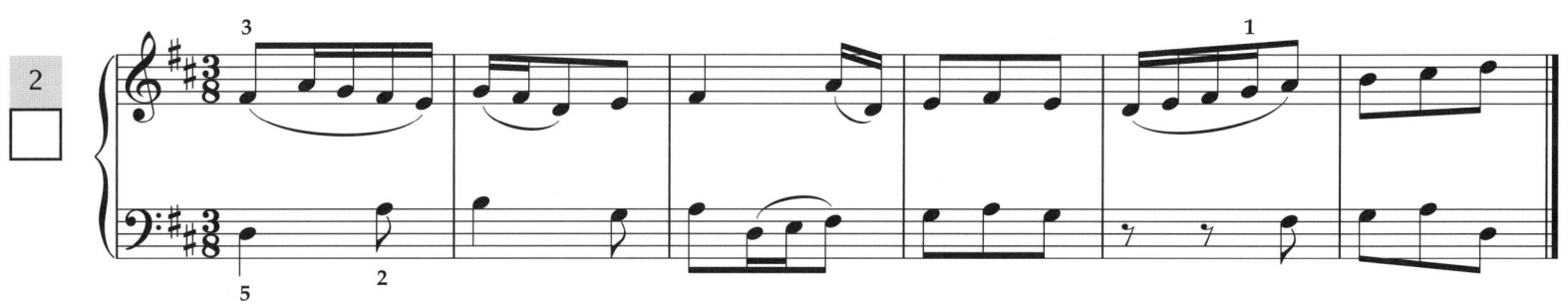

Stage 8

Prepared pieces

1. Have a brief look at this piece and decide what the character is. What leads you to your answer?
2. Can you spot any repeated patterns – rhythmic or melodic?
3. In which key is this piece? Play the scale.
4. What will you count? Tap the rhythm of each hand separately then both together.
5. Think about the fingering. Where will you have to change hand position?
6. Play the first notes in each hand and then hear the piece in your head.

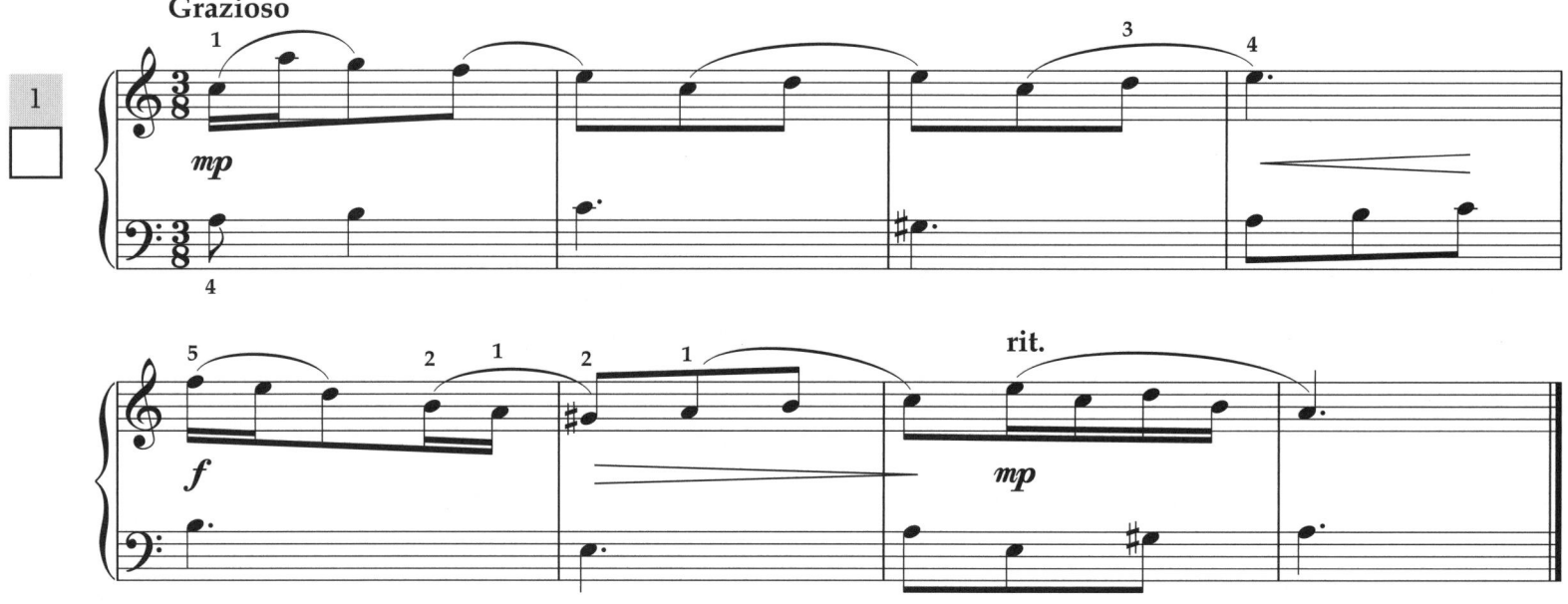

1. Think about how the character will affect the tempo you choose.
2. Can you spot any repeated patterns – rhythmic or melodic?
3. What is the key? Play the scale and arpeggio.
4. What will you count? Tap the rhythm of each hand separately then both hands together.
5. Look at the chords in the left hand bars 1-3. How will you finger them?
6. Play the first notes in each hand and then hear the piece in your head.

Going solo!

Don't forget to prepare each piece carefully before you play it.

Stage 9

Revision of keys and rhythms

Rhythmic exercises

Preparation

Here is the ideal way to prepare for sight-reading. Get into the habit of going through this checklist each time you practise your sight-reading.

1 Scan the whole piece, getting a feel for the general 'meaning'. Think about the character by noticing the various clues – tempo markings, dynamic levels, rhythm and other markings.

2 Decide what fingerings you will use at the start and notice where you will have to change hand position.

3 Try to hear the piece in your head. Don't worry about being 100% accurate – just aim to get a good overall idea of the music.

4 Feel the pulse and count in two bars before you begin.

Prepared pieces

1 Have a brief look at this piece and decide what the character is. What are the clues?
2 Can you spot any repeated patterns – rhythmic or melodic? Can you spot any scale or arpeggio patterns?
3 What will you count? Tap the rhythms of each hand separately. Then tap the rhythm of both hands together.
4 Study bars 5 and 6 for a few moments. Do you fully understand these bars?
5 Look at the chords in the right hand, bars 8-9. How are they related?
6 Play the first note and try to hear the piece in your head as best you can.

1 In what key is this piece? Play the scale and arpeggio.
2 Can you see any repeated patterns?
3 What will you count? Tap the rhythms of each hand separately. Then tap the rhythm of both hands together.
4 What do you notice about the first note in each hand?
5 What ingredients give you clues to the character of this piece?
6 Play the first note of each hand and try to hear the piece in your head as best you can.

Going solo!

Don't get your fingers in a tangle tango!

I haven't got those sight-reading blues!

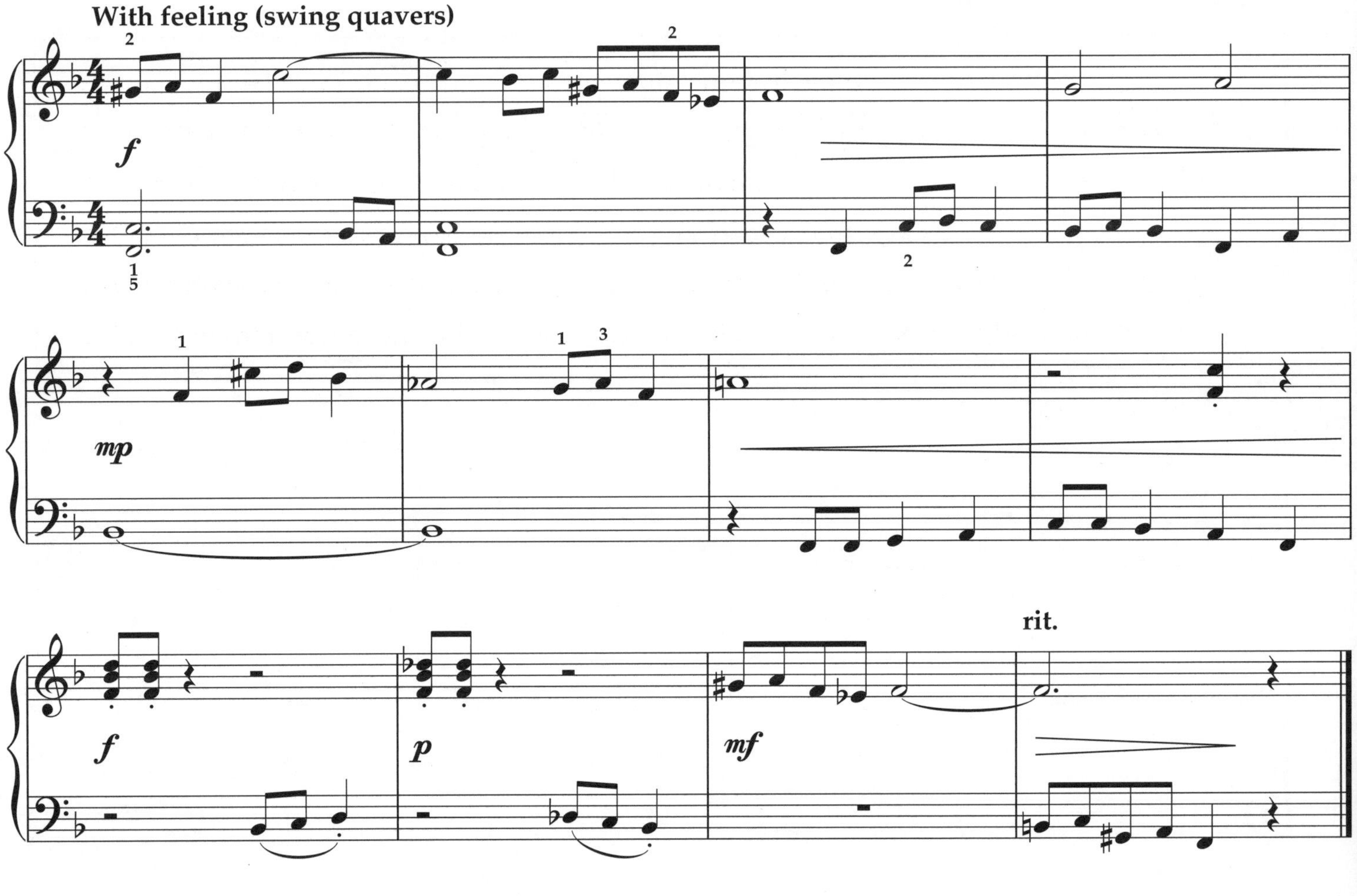